In the Field of Unintended Consequences

In the Field of Unintended Consequences

by Peter Schneider

Library of Congress Control Number: 2022923734

ISBN: 979-8-9874073-0-1

Cover Image: "Rust" by Linda Schneider
Cover Design by Glen Edelstein, Hudson Valley Book Design
Book Design by Glen Edelstein, Hudson Valley Book Design

Brooklyn and Boulder

https://www.pbandjbooks.com

For Linda

Contents

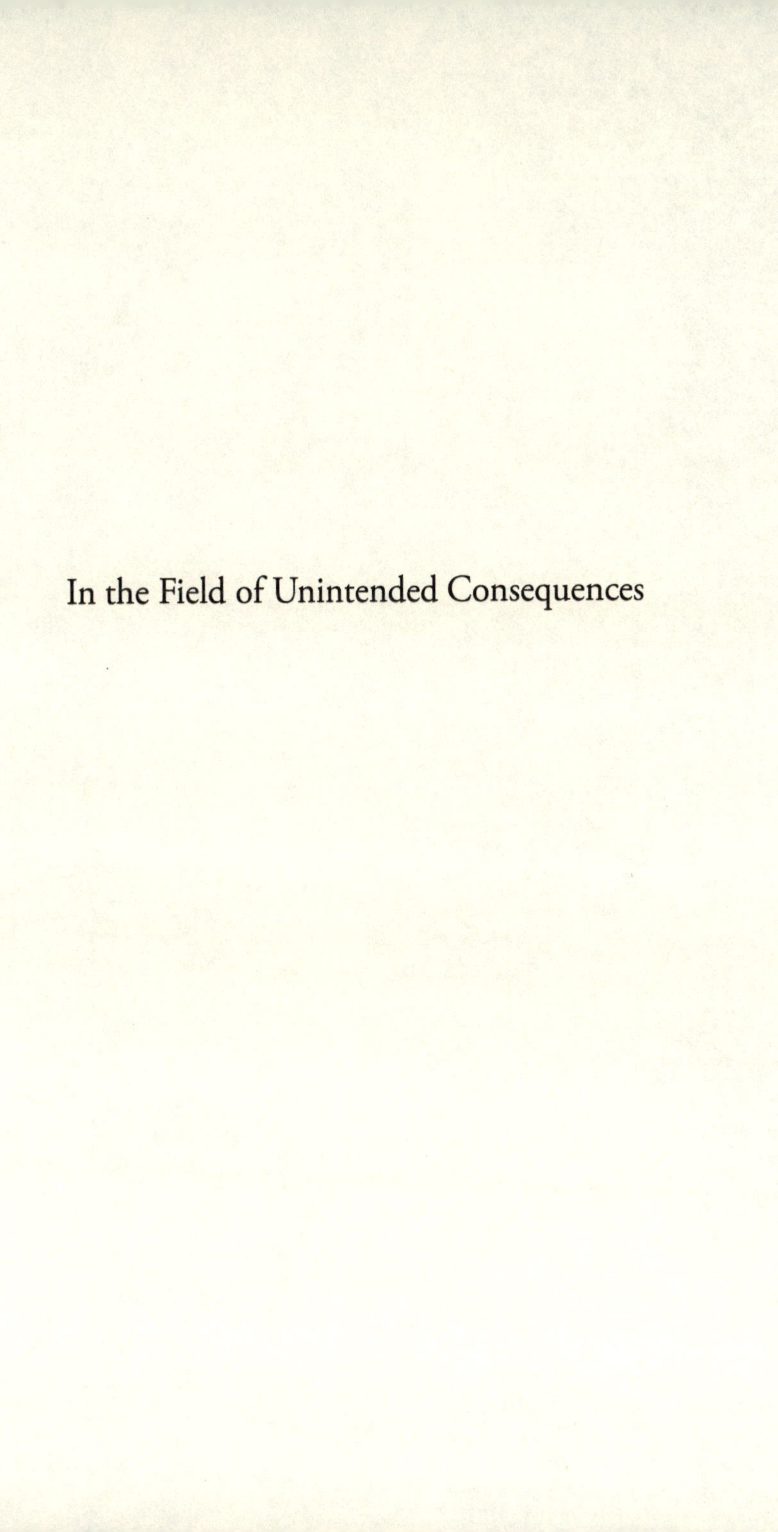

In the Field of Unintended Consequences

Wild Chervil

Invasive SOBs
white blossoms like half-popped corn
hanging over the erose spade-like leaves
stems purple when young
celery-string stalks when aged
reach through the grainy soil to anchor
at a bulbous bole of hairy root

Dug in like stubborn children
finding any crevice between the wet rocks
or hiding among ferns and grasses
in drier soil
my job this May morning
to pry them out that others may live:

bladder campion that begins in tender chartreuse
turns brown-striped with white fringe flowers
a container of vacuity cupping air
silken puffed yellow worts hug the ground
jewel weed fills old burns

joe-pye weed bluet violet
purple vetch trailing or bunched
the fierce canes of blackberry
sudden red Indian paintbrush
earthly vegetal biomass
the world's hair fresh and wet
in the morning

chervil obsessed with growth
expands its turf
like the blind economy roaring above us
and I am the small ax sharpened
to cut you down, to beat you back
capitalist imperialist weeds
depleting the common soil

And what are you?
mere micro machines of water transfer
with no purpose but to be yourselves
in ever greater profusion
like us
the mammalian niche busters
self-perpetuating perpetrators
foisted on a sleeping world

Here's the point of attack
the hori-hori   serviceable tool of ancient Japan
my samurai sword of the garden and roadside
footlong thick steel blade
halfpipe-shaped down its length

stuck-out tongue ending in a point
rectangular block of blond wood for a haft
assassin of chervil

To slip it into the gritty earth
and dig around the base:
endorphin shot to the brain
spying the purple stem
I dig down further
below the flat new leaves
and the hori-hori
GOES IN!

and down alongside
the center / searches out
the life / pries it up
the whole plant by its hairy scrotum
bole with spindly side-roots
radiating like little monkey-dicks
You're coming out of there
ya little mufuggers!
I'm extirpating your ass

THE CHERVILS ARE DEAD
the chervils are deaaaaa..d
I pulled up them suckers
now they're dead muthafuckers
deaddeaddeaddeaddeaddead
. . . .

Yeah yeah. So what?
Every spring I walk the perimeter
of my plot
and engage the enemy
a thing of equal parts
my need for order for destruction
but the chervil always wins
I clear them from the margins of our meadows
they pop up across the road
little imps with dumb white fuck-you grins

Down on Rte. 100 they're taking over whole farms
marching like medieval armies
under their white banners as in some
ridiculous Mel Gibson movie
down the roadside banks fanning out
into the fuzzy fields

And isn't it the same deal
with mental weeds
the word-and-thought chervils
ah, disingenuous me
on my black zazen cushion
plucking out what always comes back

just when I thought ("thought!")
I'd carved out
a gold patch of morning emptiness
they pull me back in….
Something comes up

a fart a pang a word
maybe I should learn
to live with them
call a truce   surrender
forget
the hori-hori
and include it all

but as A.N. Whitehead said
value lives in contrast
separation / distinction
this / not that
yay and boo
being and nothing
chervil / no-chervil
blah and blah
we value / we prefer
that is how we do

. . . .

My wife does the planting
this requires thought and planning
charting the vegetable plot
composing color
towers of flowers
our grown boys and I
supply the muscle
define an edge
pulling stubborn dandelions
levering the sober New England rocks

but rarely do I plant
that is her procreative zen
not my kind of concentration
but give me a repetitive
not completely mindless task of destruction
and a-rocking a-gouging
a-cherviling I will go
Even on a fogged-in day I am in contact
with you   wily roots
that seek the fissures between rocks
taking wicked right-angle turns
into gritty ground

and here's a sweet privacy / a secret
I am about to penetrate
yes   to extract   but first
to be in it
to be here
arbitrarily
....

I google "chervil" and
up comes the
Province of Nova Scotia website
for agriculture which says
that chervil is an invasive weed not native
to North America most likely
brought here from Britain
by means of accidental inclusion
in wildflower seed packets

now that's ironic
the very wildflowers I
am trying to free

O we humans always
wanting to improve our lot
and we succeed
in fucking things up
one way or another
. . . .

And now it's time
to treat of despair
when the chervil on the
hard-packed roadside is so small and rife
you couldn't possibly
uproot it all

what with gnats and flies
going for your eyes
landing in your ears
you've been at it as if your life
were on the line and now
you want to quit
with sweat everywhere but your mouth which is cracked
and dry
now the attack of meaninglessness
you've been fending off all morning
is upon you as you tear at the plants
creating superficial wounds in the dirt

no roots to show for it
and it's you who is hurt
while the chervil has all the time in the world
nothing to do but make trouble for us

like bankers
cooking up new ways
to crash the economy
cops
looking for reasons to kill Black people
Big Oil and industry
destroying the biosphere
righteous right-wing religious-ers
controlling women and sex and gender
on and on and on like the ten plagues of old
too many issues to tear at in desperation
and like the chervil they're always one step ahead

in Nova Scotia

and way down
in lower Westchester
traveling the parkways like meth
following the truck routes
pushing north
through Granville Gulf
attacking the moose pond sedges
and soon to be seen again
in northern Vermont and Quebec
if they're not already there

no respecter of bioregion, this stuff

and O these fucking flies and gnats
in every opening
and down the sweaty back
biting my hide
leaving little red welts
Fouahh! I try to blow them out
like thoughts that swamp
the helpless brain
So? Stop kvetching and go inside

....

The rain on the other hand
has a lesson of beauty for us
I suddenly don't care
if I'm drenched
I laugh at my city-self
who would run for cover
or stay indoors in this weather
absorption in a task is the way
to deal with the no-pleasure

I should remember this for the cushion
(fat chance)
thoughts are rain
they do as you do / if being,
be / if sleeping, sleep
if loving, love / if peeing, pee

(especially) chervil killing
is zazen   no one says
it has to be fun

So I kill you, chervil
Am I just killing time?
then why won't the thing stay dead?
O chervil I'm glad we're alive
Microphages in the gut
break down mucilaginous fibers
and I smash chervil boles into white slivers
with my hori-hori
and the monkey-dicks are crushed flat
under the passing tires
killing to give life
to the cornflower
the summer aster
sedges / ferns / grasses
all imbricate   tangled up with each other
blue / orange / lavender

Eros and Thanatos
from the floor tiles of
the new house going up
covering over the breathing shale

from the bright red nematodes
at garden's edge
to the miles of asphalt that flowed
from the well of Titusville

to encircle the globe
and choke the weeds
and deprive us of home
sure   life kills / it's a phage
and chervil is just one phase
good bad / neither both

So then, what are its uses?
could these roots be cooked?
pounded boiled sautéed
fried until their bitterness
is disguised by human invention
spice and butter
animal fat and heat

the older plants
sour the cattle's silage
when they go to seed
but the Brits call it "cow parsley"
"the bright white sign of
English Summer"

good to eat
but not to confuse with
fool's parsley which will poison
or hemlock which will kill
while the taste of garden chervil
is somewhere between
parsley and fennel

and the scrotal root also
is edible when boiled
or soaked in rice water
a general tonic"
"a healing weed"

Chervil, I'm sorry
but I'm still afraid to eat you
and since no one around here
will eat you either
I'll have to keep on killing
because you are invasive
like thoughts   like itches
like words   like obsessions

and because I need to
see the little bluets
peeking through the ground cover

then it's invade the invader
because I'm invasive too
like all my kind / and, yes
the planet would be better off without us
but then, who'd keep down the chervil?

After a rain when it's fresh
these chervils, so eager to live
in their white frankness, it's easy
to imagine them on a morning without us

their future stick-like deadness
seems just a theory / tweedy ugly
bundles-to-be at the edge of my hairy meadows
where persistent recurrent waves ripple through
O how anonymous and unknowable
is any given moment
particularly without us

that dead branch over there
splayed out like a besom
and the purple stems of chervil
have entered my dreams
it's a little sickening
like why I gave up fishing

living among dying worms
and tearing the hook from soft mouths
but I still eat fish
hypocrite householdeur.

It's time to stop / turn around / take stock
the chervil's not going away
and I'm not either just yet
for sure it will outlast me
hang on after my little snit
my spare-time campaign /
little piddleshit ripple
on the surface of biological events
neither of us comprising the bulk
of the biomass / that honor

belongs to the bacteria
but today it seems possible the total weight
of the world's chervil is more than
the mass of the world's humans

and a pile of dead
chervil stalks / roots / leaves
associated soil and pebbles
is surprisingly heavy
just try hauling it up to the road
from a little way down in the field

try hauling around big ideas
or numbers like the total biomass
or all of the dead and you'll
get tired pretty fast

and then there's the question of how to dispose
of chervil numbers or ideas
in poem or prose
or life

My neighbor Frank comes by to say
his method is to pour gasoline on the pile
and light it but I don't want to go that way too industrial
after this labor-intensive ferreting
and I'm sure I'd start a fire

One year I packed them in black bags
threw them over a stone wall in the woods

fearing they might escape
like ideas or poems
that get away from you and create
associative jungles

Some of my neighbors commend this fight
the high-minded minister and his high-minded wife
but the rich lady on the hill doesn't
want to drive over the roots
and regular folk tell me
it will cause motorcycle accidents
on wet roads   so
I move the chervil
closer to the verge

But as for myself I just don't know
is it an escape, an avoidance
to focus on the one weed
when the true invaders are
the mind weeds?
On any given day as I fall
subject to assaults
from the vaults of nameless nothing
this white-capped intruder
is a too-convenient opposition
and we're locked in a war of attrition

Yet at times the forces align
the body / the weather / the mind
give a brief opening to delight

and pulling chervil seems wholesome
harmless and nothing like a fight
. . . .

My wife understands natural selection
better than I and points out
trees / birds / plants / animals / everything's
invasive until checked
by the next contender

Should I wait
for natural balance to take hold
and stop my chervil-pulling bender?

Nah, I need to see the campion
before the summer's out

The wall of pines across the meadow
is really a shell around a core of hardwoods
growing up at their feet

less invasion than succession
for years I have heard their conversation
from my window and seen it in
the orchestrated gestures of wind
choreographed prayers to the inevitable

The mind coiling around itself
generating pasts / sinks down

into sussurance / sedimented silences
solemn cathedral aisles of noble nonsense

Mornings after a storm
the meadow and wall of trees
are freshened   every edge
every distinction thrums
the chervil is white and beautiful

the poem I have been waiting for all spring
keeps almost arriving
from where?
the mailbox at the end of the drive
under the pillow
down the well?

poem composed in equal parts
of mind-spume and air
delight delusion despair
chervil living and thriving
the cracks in the plenum of now
the moment to look
into every being without venom
to lift eyes from book
ground and stone and stare
into the middle distance
at no goal

Momentous events are happening elsewhere
bullshit and death in the news
while chervil marches over the earth
here where at least it is wet and secret
and the humans are reasonably spaced

Annelids of the garden
tender coiling threads
through the breathing plenum
help me   I don't know how
. . . .

Any given plant like any given word
is embedded in a tangle of its companions
the sea of language
the Mato Grosso of meaning and cross-meaning
and the poem floating on top of it
epiphenomenal   so vulnerable
can always be chopped down like chervil
or pulled up by the root
and what would we have then?

O chervil waving in the breeze
you really are innocent and sometimes beautiful
(I suppose)

but ugly and redundant
as you clump swarm and multiply
need I draw the obvious analogy
between beautiful and too much?

the supermarket pyramids
of produce in their shine
the excess of structure in
oil tanks cranes and junkyards
of derelict equipment along the
New Jersey Turnpike
a hundred miles of robot vomit

or those cancer cells
recently resident in my body?
Same deal with them
they just wanted to live
like chervil and everything else
but not at my expense you little fuggers
we rooted you out too

too bad I had to lose a part of
this self   my little prostate
no bigger than a walnut or an almond
and where is it now?
preserved in a jar
for future consultation?
in a landfill on Staten Island?

or like my chervil
decomposing in a black bag
thrown over a stone wall
in the dank woods behind the house
And no one can pretend
that shit doesn't happen

that the big world doesn't exist
even in a small hollow like mine
come little annoying facts
cancer and loss

and goddam WILD CHERVIL!

All that   and Japanese knotweed
opioids heroin and meth
in Randolph and Rutland coming up
the Connecticut valley / desperate users
clipping car parts for the catalytic converters
a few bucks worth of platinum / stripping
copper wiring from houses
while nineteenth century farms
persist up dirt roads tucked into folds
on the state map
. . . .

Then let the pretty weeds get together
in Kropotkinian mutual aid
unlike this foolish human
staggering around stabbing the ground
with my hori-hori
miserable and dumb
as wrists sprain and thumbs
and back protest
Dude, you don't have to do this
you're not a migrant farm worker
not a desperate subsistence gardener

in parched Madagascar
though someday you may be one

But then, who will be responsible?
Of course there's always the State
the State that spreads the weeds
by mowing late after they've gone to seed
and lets them mature so that
they also propagate by root

they fucked us up, the Highway Dept.
they didn't mean to do it but they did

and yet if they mowed early
they would cut down my other beauties
O what to do, what to do?
It's the field of unintended consequences
the friggin practico-inert
the humans banded together
to co-operate and postpone individual death
first came the hunt and gather
then the slash and burn
next the accumulative agriculture
surplus and priests / warriors and chiefs
and what do we get?
bullshit and death
and stupid little things
like runaway chervil

but even now
I can take the side of chervil
because their dumb persistence is
so much like ours

Francis Ponge
sided with things /
personified the pinewoods
he hid in during the war

while the light shone
through his enclosures
so unlike the war photos / raw
black and whites
of mud, mechanism and rubble

Maybe he could inhabit these meadows
chervil and knotweed
emerald ash borers bluebottle and
bog-dwelling lady slipper
startling in its enclosure
avens' spikes with sticky dew
seminal drops / clotted bio-mascara
all the improbable plants in
Darwin's tangled bank / the loving community

until we see they're all caught up in war
progress and retreat
today   the chervil has its way
tomorrow   the next superpower

Beaver ponds in the gulf
disappear under a slow assault of sedges meadows
hemmed in by hedges / soon
paved over for car lots and big box stores

while fields of Indian paintbrush
still exist as do earlier versions
of ourselves up at Shrewsbury
youths lying in love in a summer meadow

moods compete and turn invasive
preference for one type of memory
over another / one self over another
ideals somewhat arbitrary compete with each other
going stale when one of them wins
all things invasive until meeting the competitor
the killer inside bacterial microphage cancer time
It's time to face the
No-game emptiness
The Great Empty the Tao
and who then can be the True Man
or Woman of No Rank?
. . . .

Galaxies quasars pulsars black holes
subatomic ur-plasma before the bang

is there competition among these
a universal law of fitness / survival of
and fit for what? Being, eh?

and what does that compete with?
all these distinctions locally OK
destruct on contact

just like this rant and where did
it come from? where
does it belong? right here
where it sprouted
like a bunch of crappy chervil
no narrative no argument no gloss
although there is fall and loss / no
obvious agent no redemption
no end / just
progress and retreat
the repetitive tasks of weeding out

as the old Roshi said
we must sit and cut down the thought-weeds
and pile them up next to
next to...
the MIND!
(whatever that is)

and do it again

Quilted Pillows

A gooey mat of microbes covered the seafloor at the time,
and on that blanket lived a variety of enigmatic animals
whose bodies resembled thin, quilted pillows.

—Douglas Fox: "What Sparked the Cambrian Explosion?" *Nature* 2/10/2016

1.
and this is how I developed the habit
of inhabiting a body
a habitance that keeps
breaking up and reforming
a one-body problem
a one and a many
until you showed up
fractalizing and scintillating my edges
into greater unions and losses

pale sun breaking through formations
arguments for being fill the liquid plain
a letter a sail a conversation
going to Rome for no reason
code coding against white sky
this this and this

successive instigations
miracle-ing up from quilted pillows

Utica in the rain
cold ideas spiraling down
from the train to the wooded bottom
left behind in upstate New York
a bed of coelacanths   fossilized industry
fields folded into thin slabs
like vast quilted pillows

vectors of events
with language splaying over
codes diploid / haploid
ever widening regions
brackets / molds / annelids / analogues
sticks in water in green sunlight
we drift toward each other we frictionate

under the watch
of long slow molecular millennial clocks
societies and societies of societies
singing to themselves

and now it is the market / the god
who determines all things
plummeting to the ground to spread
the skittered brown
commentary of leaves

an accumulated history
stomata / cups

2.

Deuterostomic, we barely know
one hole from another
exchange's prototype with no rest
breath rattles the chest
this is not a test
everything happens in concrescent crests
love in our bed
of quilted pillows

voices far away snatch at a tune
out of the rain
vapors over a stunned sea

to sing about it
sing   sing out of my mind
now my teeth   my gut
my eyes blinkered blind
a dazzle of microbial spores
congeries of sensations
tracks and trucks of Chinese vegetables

commerce at noon
I temporally locate
focally dissolve
in the market solvent to all exchange

gliding conversations

the signature, aim, and name of our epoch
like   like   like

as Whitehead said,
Propositions are a lure for feeling.
What? What the fuck?
yes / precisely / the fuck

commerce and rot
Koreatown hallucinatory foulness
in old doorways back hallways
ground into the green linoleum
hand trucks of vegetal Verwesung
Ver-the decay   the turning as Trakl did say

in his verwirrt und wahnsinnig way

but, love, it is love
like the fresh bicycle
chained to a railing in the sun
late afternoons of noise receding
quilted pillows falling   grieving

like and unlike the even hum
of air conditioners   filters and siphons
stacks of servers the blue servant savants
in their windowless concrete shells
at the city's edge

and yet even such as these
are more entropic
than all the vegetables of this world

the calm order of disorder
of love as it is   "the objective
immortality of the previous moment"
Whitehead calls it "god's activity
whoever the hell s(he) it is
however s(he) it happens

3.

you
a poem
a pole
an accretion
a dust
an attribution

watch
the distance between
distances close
always infinitesimally close
swift adhesion of quilted pillows
you put together a universe
too busy to rehearse
a set of events a subset of primes
how we relate

falling chimes of intention
poised on cusps
I'm staring at you
you're staring at me
our gazes copulate
networks of mutual attention

what is gained by exchange
(no bdelloid rotifers we)
I clone nothing without your world
this null intertwined with textures / quiltings
mysterious fabrics / the smallest possible length

thus and so that your voice
un-separates from mine
your heat your heart
amplifies mine
an argument for each other
we presuppose each other's each

now if we reach into a field
and soak up every green phenomenon
trees in their parrot-feather childhood
the green and bleached mulch

interwoven
the hormic formic urges
of our cousin ants
and no one is uninvited

to the stretched out unfolding dance
the little annelids and fleshy purple worms
in plentiful accordance aspects of lovely chance
these seen from the air
form vast mats
quilted pillows
of summation
the hollows repeat
imbricate recursive equations
a loud cumulative shout emerges
from a bed of silence

an explosion in the mind
of Whitehead's god
which is you
and you and you and
me into each other
the fucking forward of time
living by the one geometry
self-quilting   auto-connecting
and the falling off
the dying

4.

quilted pillows selfless softly settled
on the seafloor way before any sea shells
in tonight's heat we sift through each other's
histories / sediments / moisture drying on each

out the back rhythmic repetitions of yards and streets
it is Brooklyn / now a throaty pulse humming / rising
air vents or traffic conversations of the public world
the sadness of the now   a point open to the past

open to the past / a barren coast at sunset
new suburbs count themselves in dopplering light
a succession a decision of roofs / eyelike windows
litter the ridges and soon it is San Francisco

open to the past on a golf course at night
in the suburbs lying with another
confused hope / torn-up self straining toward a future
open to the past which refuses to close down

opens past death this membranous breath
the interfusion the interpretive buzz
of dusk now cued up in a Vermont hollow
light at the horizon / a radio awareness

a thread / a creode / a character / not a self
morphing through harmonic stages
any place or being not itself never itself
a performance an exhibition

of ecstatic historic sadness
the city in spring / brick walks
the helpless layered quilting of things just so

5.

One azalea flower presents itself
gravely gaudy against
the gas green sky at dusk

we cup cherry blossom bunches
we cup each other's faces
all moments quiver

every spring we return to hear
a distant roar
the crowd in history

a bicycle chained to a black fence
stunned to frankness
in sunlight
now
the breath resumes its pulsation
one…

6.

brown and white pigeon
cow-like mutation
released from sleep
startles up from my
quilted pillow

psittacine head
grazes my cheek and fingers
flaps the room twice
and we let it out

to the dense smoked gray
woods behind the house
vectoring… vectoring
what we do all day

7.

nothing speaks except
with its authentic voice
in the massive brick mausoleum
apartments at river's edge

electricity on all the time
a solo pianist in a box in the sky
playing sonatas / sodalities of sound
drifting down to the barren grounds
like quilted pillows

acknowledge in their descent
seabirds whirling over the river
conflicting currents
engage at the tip of the island

surrounding neighborhoods
in convocation / the cliffs

of buildings formally address
each other

the crowd sulks and shines
lets out a regional sigh
the descendants of quilted pillows
insist on their silence

8.

sensing a crack in the rock
beings such as us seek
to emerge from emulsion
this is the compulsion
of the quilted pillows' career
kings of bladder emptiness

Pythagorean beans
in a beany universe
it is good

to dig into soil
and stick and bang
against the glinty shale

to hollow out holes
and deliver
the little white seeds

9.

then we were in the green laboratory
shafts of mote-filled light streaming
through dirty windows
lined up on high metal tables
in blocks of translucent green glass
societies of quilted pillows

an inch across or even smaller
self-replicating raviolis suspended
in the crystalline medium

no one was shouting but now
a consensual idea took form in the air
under the rows of halogen lamps

You You You You You
You have done this
Do you have anything to say?

about the different orders under formation
differentiation / off-branching indifferent
deadends and destruction   tell us tell us

what you intend
we the quilted pillows are organized
we have a right to know

Openings

1. Sitting

Upright / I am a collection under a skin

cities districts highways piled
on themselves
concrete shelves and balconies
old slate pavements
over the undulating mantle

nothing is a statement
montages of corsages and garages
motor starting up in the chest

2. Word in Body

You invested in words that meant something
a definite process like rye bread
or Mozart in the dentist's office

a barometric dip
a shift in density
water falling away

in back of the human gesture
our glances slide over each other
machined to a fine tolerance

3. Awakeness

Lost bones lying in the dark
the act of saying
just one need among many
to carry a faint tablet
toward morning
4. Abandoned Woods

Neglected scrub wood
behind the garden apartments
place of secrecy and skunk cabbage

where the barelegged children went
in summer to be left alone
with something they could not express
on the clipped lawns under the oaks

a concrete culvert below the road
brown trickle running down its center
they thrust out arms and legs
pentangling through to light

5. Opening / Closing

And so we fail and fail again
to attend to the ghostly hoo-ing
scattered points in the field
a mourning dove? a hunting owl? a wedge
a shim in the black laminates of evening

and it is "I" the one who sees
his father's face in the mirror
the death mask, the jaw set
in characteristic shit-eating grin
jellied eye quavering voice

6. You Are a Stranger

you are familiar
each other's strange familiar
"My wife"
what does this mean
skin touch / voice touch / an opening

7. Dark / Empty

not to forget
to go out to inspect
the jeweled net of Indra

this night among billions of brilliances
we are cold and hug on the porch

lips graze neck as restless mind
seeks mammalian warmth

8. Obscenity of the Chair

the trajectory of the chair
an Adirondack chair and how it came
to be there
plunked down in tired wasted woods
splayed out at the railroad embankment

9. Quietus

Bonnefoy, French poet,
returns to a New England graveyard
cream-colored clapboards
catch the late afternoon light
maples firing up
gray headstones
sink deeper into greenness
erase thoughts of the everyday
permit us to say One

10. OK, Let's Say It

One

One / one / one / one / one

1
    1
        1
1
    1
a reticule of ones / a
net of non's

for an opening to dissolve

a queen's pawn poem to
queen's (k)night three or zero captured
en passant
this could be one's koan

11. Density

an aspirational opening
the best trick / the best trip
the one when you don't know
where you're going
when you jumped off the train to scramble

through the thickets
calligraphic darts across a field
no closure / an opening in the wind
slaps you full on
a cliff in space

12. View

black foliated hill piling up
out of a high meadow
a bluish gray building mountaining
at the edge of a city neighborhood

many lives in green-lit corridors
the thud of the day accumulates
chimerical incinerator shaft

13. Trail

An opening in the white quartz
moss-covered cliff
water sweetening the walls
of the rock crevice / stony vagina
an old friend I always revisit
on the trail to Mt. Abraham summit

and here is the sky opening to the southwest
the rhythm of hills leading into the world
down the Eastern corridor
distant car schmutz / a floating hawk

14. The Thirst

always the thirst
for the other reality

behind / between / alongside

unnoticed in the career of a life
spent staring into space

nothing real
leading away from nothing real
meadowsweet furzy pasture
black wall of trees
winking in and out of existence
accumulated irony
of lichen-covered rock

Black Garnet

Inhabiting
bare granite summits of Vermont
you find them

on Mansfield / Camel's Hump / Lincoln
and Hunger mountains / hard tight black seeds
set into the gray green igneous swirl

easily mistaken for fungus or lichen
deceptive in tenacity
try to pry one out / it resists

very occasionally you can abrade
a flaking weathered outcrop
and rub one free

dull black speck
in your palm
self-contained / reluctant

yielding a highlight
under the influence of
your sweat

black garnet like a perfect found
poem quarried out of
emptied mind

peeking out from piles
of old words / figure against the ground
the making   really an extracting

China

1.

my Brooklyn ceiling fan this humid August
reminds me of one years ago in
an upstairs north Jersey Cantonese restaurant
"Old Shanghai"

dirty fish-tank green walls /
fan distributing flies
a few desultory patrons

an old man in a very white shirt
came with our subgum chow mein
and cokes in little glasses

two crew-cut brothers
two bucks each for dinner out
on a school night

the knobbed metal dome over the serving dish
a beautiful mystery
lost numinosities / the rest is history

2.

in Burton Watson's translation class
the high lonely purity
of Wang Wei first revealed itself

Burt kind and gentle
read our translations then his own
and finally the shocking original

issuing from a place
way back in his throat
or from the middle of his shiny skull

despairing lust overtook me then
as I gazed at the class's girls
in the heat haze of late New York spring
imagining the ivory and rose bodies
under their cotton dresses

3.

alone in San Francisco
I wandered down to the park
by the Embarcadero
to see the parrots

when a woman / grande dame of parrots /
wearing high rubber boots
perhaps a bit deranged
gave me some bird food

I held it in two tins
arms outstretched
and soon was covered in parrots

well-mannered birds
perched on my bare head and shoulders
like a line of little houses on a distant city ridge
not one scratched or shat

the TV crew came to film us
then I climbed back up to Chinatown
through fish-smelling streets
to a fish-smelling alley off of Grant

up the stairs of an old wooden building
like an open cardboard box to a restaurant
one story up / window perched over the street
empty inside
they served noodles in fish paste
ahh…real Chinese food, says I /
food of the people

4.

sent by Tai Chi teacher Sifu Chen
to a bookstore on Mulberry north of Canal
to get a treatise on the Taoist Chi Gong

but everything was in Chinese
and no one was there

wandered upstairs knocking on doors
pushed one open and lo
a real dojo all Chinese men
and a few women doing push-hands

that was the genuine wu shu
family secrets
not taught to blue-eyed devils
they turned to stare

5.

"China" to a white guy
all construct and disappearing essence

I used to think
I wanted to go there
to visit the hermits
in the mountains
now maybe not

what with the oppression
and filthy particulate air

but in the past
the Old Shanghai still lives
and the real wu shu is
wu wei and everywhere

Springs

Water pours from the god's mouth out of the pale rock
in a grove near Oppidum / Oppide en Gaule.
Heat shimmers / mind wavers / tongue desires
shade in afternoon dust.

Classical violence.

Centuries later my ancestors made it back east
from Spain to Macedonia; who knows how?
They might have walked right by
this little ville en France
men behind carts blinking dumbly at the ruins
head-scarved woman suckling a child.

Slogging the coast to Marseille
to Nice and on into Italy Florence / Trieste
on to the Dalmatian coast and inland over wolvèd
mountains to Monastir stopping arbitrarily.

Or maybe at sea in a square boat
to Genoa down to Palermo and around Sicily
to Salonika…

Grain dealers and money lenders with Serbian
passports made it to New York.
Turkinos of the Grand Concourse
with their heavy gold inkwells, brass jizvehs,
loukum and baklava developing the family craziness
the Sephardic hysteria.

 Now I'm here / arbitrary remnant
 standing by a New England roadside spring
 worn smooth / iron spout anchored in granite.

From these filtering soils the mind
prepares as ground and forgets
what it has proposed

whispers of the heaviness of being
of boredom, insomnia
and the night watching itself.

Gods mist up from the slough
below the roadbed
words follow clumping along
intimate in their distance.

As in the Tuscan hills the wind
catches up a wall of trees
churning the limbs in choreography
in conversation in orchestration
in prayer to the inevitable.

From the Book of
Numinous Dreams

1.

Marble lobby hundreds of feet high
green clerestory windows / golden
elevators rising and descending

you enter the chased jewel box
press a number / pass your floor
and burst through the roof

the glass car careens around
on a silver rail in the black tar
you look off in all directions
a brick city / vined terraces
covered by awnings

people line up on walkways
in the rain
the feeling too subtle to label
fear / elation / smallness / distance

the elevator car descends by another chute
discharged into the lobby
you press another button

2.

A hotel's
plush dark red atrium
Viennese chandeliers

you walk through turning corridors
and open what seems to be a broom closet
to find yourself sleeping inside
tucked out of the way
forgotten
fucked

3.

Long bus ride out of the city
over an iron bridge
past scrap metal yards

broken pavement / wooden shacks
canting in toward each other
papers blowing in a mild April wind

hypertext to an elevated roadway
heat rising from your body

4.

A psychedelic green lizard
is licking a baby's face
the baby laughing
suddenly overwhelmed
starts to cry
Stop it snakey / silly snakey

5.

Presentation of lakes
blue stages on a path
over the earth's curvature
beyond the first wall of the mountains

fine needles of northern spruce
branches wet and black
steam rising from the thick red pine duff
a path furrowing lower

6.

to a rock road, a stream bed
in the Orinoco basin
the car bounces down a series of
crumbling stone steps
vines closing in darkness

then you are out on a razor-like bridge
slanting downward into the water
a phrase repeats itself /
the one and the many

7.

Room with velvet walls
the sallow old man in a black robe
devotees ranged in ranks
you watch all silence
as faces elongate

in another sector hand to hand
combat on the parapets
swords skimming geometric
precise arcs
slitting throats

8.

Running through other people's lives
fenced backyards and suburban lawns
doors / windows / porches
you enter a house and hear
muffled voices behind walls

down wooden stairs
to a long corridor

the smell of fresh concrete,
pipes / old desks / dust

a gray metal door
shuts behind you and you drift
in a vast underground garage
trucks thrumming

9.

What's his name?
Mr. Badanes
Well, he up and gone
disappeared

and came out on a steep white embankment
boulders along the highway
slabs of gray sky

he was talking some stuff
about life's turbidity / viscosity /
the concept of torque /
but I'm not going out to look for him
or his discarded conversations

10.

After the flood a set of ruined books
wet pages rippled
cross-sectional

infoldings of sandwich meat
along the river
there is a tearing in the wind
and a tearing in the eyes

lines of human figures
stretch stick-like
to the horizon

11.

Now the coyotes' chorale swells
and wavers through the hollows
in Vermont hill country

transforms across the silent barrier
to the country of sleep
into a silken flowing of the voiceless
gray-eyed whippets

they drive me down
through the valley
moon
casting cold films on the waters

12.

A car glides in the night
along a black-paved street
crests a hill as the pavement

cracks and pours toward a tunnel
that becomes a square conduit
metal bands frame white
mother-of-pearl casing
devastated light of a hotel corridor
anxiety in the green patterned carpet

Car hits a wall and you get out and walk
down the hall / the ranks of doors
recede to a vanishing point

hollow drumming in the overhead pipes
sudden turns / twisting camera pans /
walls closing in now / narrow / interrupted
by spans and catwalks / a ship's passageways
the smell of greasy soup
everyone at their stations

pool attendants offer hot towels
steam rising from the green water
cashiers in cubicles
shoeshine men at marble stands

in the solarium nude women
brown and smoothly draped
over chaises / menacing invitations /
a purple silk bookmark
trailing out of a dark vulva

someone has turned on the meaning machine
and the letters
                        E
      L   T   R
        A
roll from everyone's mouth
in flat rippled skywriting

Letter to Space

the attacks of meaninglessness are getting worse
but in this certainly I am not alone
mine take the form of a Huh? spot about two inches
below the top of my cranium and an inch and a half or so
in from the forehead

impulses have gone viral literally
not to mention that with one cosmic methane fart from
the permafrost
we're planet Venus.
So goodbye this little human consciousness / mine
and yours and everyone we know and don't
who will die of microbe or virus
in hospital or at home alone or not
and without these minds will the universe
become one big undifferentiated block?

Maybe yes but maybe no given the extremely high
odds of other civilizations
that will posit / differentiate / objectivate / love (?)

whatever
but then probably kill themselves
if they haven't already

Some lunatic billionaire should
send up a capsule with the complete recordings of Bud
Powell   so any intelligences out there
will know we did make something great

and you can fill in your preferred cultural artifact
here______

<blockquote>
"Everywhere men speak in
whispers I brood on the
uselessness of letters"

—Tu Fu
</blockquote>

Han Shan wrote poems
in the weather
on rocks and cliff walls
on boulders in the rain

the record does not say
what implement he used
maybe a long dry stick
with a burnt charcoal end

while in Tu Fu's storm
the years fall like snow
buried poems breathe under the crust
and out in the universe
huge entities are clashing

galaxies / pulsars / black hole systems
eating each other / one is moved

to think of it not as terrible ultimate annihilations
but childish contests of movie dinosaurs

with no sound or
medium of transmission
nothingness versus nothingness
no hearers

Han Shan's silent poems
washed away by rain
as much a sound or shout
as any cosmic process

Tu Fu's storm holds his modest whisper
and I am struck by the vanity / the sadness /
the bathos of dragging this pen
across this page

while my realm destroys itself
much as did the High Tang
under his bereft gaze

The Coraçon Function

She was a former nun
large and very white
and I was among

her terrified students
in high school mathematics
as the wooden room resounded
with her brass voice.

If you got it, she could become
friendly if such a word applied

No, friendly is not accurate
rather a hot numerical passion
a furious zeal

and one day I got it
or so I thought
the coraçon function
generating a heart shape

turned on its side
burgeoning out from origin
a string of numbers dragging a small
body twisting around itself

with a peculiar sideways gravity
on the graph paper

Fifty and more years later
lying on my side in the cardiac unit
I rejoin this equation

and recall how she sang La Vie en Rose
at the faculty talent show
while I accompanied her on piano

not her best student, I
remember the wine-colored taffeta dress
the tight brown curls framing

her pearl-toned face
upturned nose
perched above a massive body

Ah Miss Cotter dear Maggie
I'm sure you're gone now
and I'm still here

with this strange thing inside me
a sloshing whumping function

Philosophy Library

The idea of it
after so many years
no There there anymore
no more tables the color of a well-baked pretzel
oak grains with blackened grooves
thin wooden ladders reaching up
over iron balconies past the ranks of books
preserved lives of trees and ancient dead thoughts
leather topped desks replaced now
by ugly blocky carrels and screens

O you books and books
and myself a young man
barely past childhood
trying to puzzle out the Greek from context
absorbing mystic senses and propositions
from all that wood
the green student lamps
and enveloping chairs

falling asleep over Bergson and Husserl
at war with Russell's theory of types
I get it I don't get it I get it! I don't get it

My lover, you couldn't understand then
how I could possibly care about this bullshit
but now have come to accept it
which I am not even sure that I do anymore
but no matter I have no choice
the questions recur like a toothache
a self-feeding asymptote

Meanwhile there are real stories out there
about sex and power,
oppression, the identities,
and the casual cruelties of this veteran planet

while in here Heraclitus keeps stepping
into a nameless river falling endlessly away
many more times than twice and Pythagoras
runs past his bogeyman bean field to die

The books in colored columns
are pipes of a silent organ
heterogeneous collections
entities
and so one sees
there is no good reason
why things matter
just that they do

Gingko and footnotes

Gingko full in fall
yellow chains and bunches
on black wet branches*

Cascade of jewels / chimes of glass
and thick fractality of petals
greeny yellow on the path*

A presence a presence
the tree and its leavings
gathering ambient light*

and vomit smell*
of smashed fruit*
on the ground

*An initial approximation, yes, but what of the carpets
their composition and further career?
These delicate ladies
fluttering in the gutter behind their fans mingle

with tawny disillusioned oak leaves
cigarette butts and the opaque rubber ring tops
of used condoms / the alien etiolated whiteness
of candy wrappers Ah! Ayi! a black hump
dead rat or discarded face mask fragment
of our North American disaster and urban wabi-sabi

Pick up one of these fan-creatures warm to the touch
like skin against your human skin
sentience to sentience
yellow in the sun and the little grooves
articulate their nature
plant? animal? like ourselves consecutive
corpuscular

but soon this carpet compacts and molds
after the first rain
brews a brunello distillation on the way to dissipation
annihilation before the further remains

*the vomit-fruit coral-pink under a mottled white film
like glaucous eyeballs or damaged testicles
and the last stems / little threads / skeletal dusts

*seen through a window the branches appear
as a specimen on a slide / micro-limbs of infusoria
arbitrarily selected denominated ganglia
but… return to the whole and just look at it
look at it, bro, look at the fucking tree
the gray-grooved bark / the trunk

wood-perfect in its achievement
green vines growing up the thick shaft
shy and hopeful pubic hairs
they do / they twine / they dare
in the raw autumn air

*Pools (poets) of color (gold)
rooms of echoing fractality
soundings of bathos oh yeah
my scattered heart my tattered
destroyed self / the winter gingko
of black branches / spikes /
mathematical markings
apportioning space and time
in the moving immensity
the city as mechanism / organism
organic mechanism / mechanical organism
we helpless beings
so many wants in its wash

and the gingko involved in it
ambassador of time condensing
its breathing (our breathing)
ongoing being at imperceptible
warp speed and if we really see it
we join it we be it

information transmitted /
the color infuses every interior
gold shock to the eye
black wetness in the gut

branches in the wind
skreak against each other
bring the hearer to a point

the inquiring whine of the pi-pa
offset by Mozartean fillibrations
petals / habits / our home / our innards
all displayed in public
vomit-smell of smashed fruit on the ground*
the gingko naked as us
and subject to the city's constraints

We are told that the gingko is among the oldest species
on earth having appeared on Laurasia
in the middle Jurassic before the continents split
now almost extinct in the wild it has been cultivated
for thousands of years
first in China then Korea and Japan
object of Taoist/Buddhist veneration
and now here in public on 9th Street Brooklyn, USA

We are told that it is hardy and thrives
in semi-wild borderlands like 9th Street
suspended in a miasma of gas fumes
shit and piss of passing dogs
collective wailing of sirens and shouts
to all of which it remains impervious
or even welcoming and defiant
but dignified / above

*ginkgo…
just living its life
private in public
like this room of yellow light
and books suspended
in the organic mechanism
of the city

intersection of cars / shouts / trees
cyclical circuit
of the old / the fast / the slow
a ginkgo caught up
in the universal whirl
and we climb down it
and keep descending
the now
lifts and drops

like these branches
lift and droop
in a gesture
of play-the-pi-pa

(Old Tai Chi teacher Da Liu
said: We do not care for fighting
we play the Tai Chi Chuan
for health
health, longevitay
and beautay)
crazy, yes?

the gingko also ripples with chi
But what was it we meant to establish?
That the ginkgo lives among humans
in a strange dependency
having been tamed
maybe even saved

yet maintains its indifference
to our discontinuities
conversations in bars
interrupted by plague

words drifting out of doors
and floating up in thick night air
encircle the tree but mean little
to the ginkgo
its time and silence
not of our measure

We are told that trees
communicate with their kind
through roots and underground rhizomes
maybe so
but the ginkgos of 9th Street
seem taciturn at their bases
reserving their expression
for the upper stories
*a gold fanning out in fall
dense darkening green in heat-time
*wet black bones in the snow

the bare branches are covered
with nubbly nodes
for measurement? judgment?
commenting on our obsessive need
for order / interval / distinction

but the limbs themselves
nonquantitative beautifully curling
flowing as in the Tai Chi Chuan
(old teacher Da Liu, etc.) / ah
these trees / the living health
longevitay and beautay

You object to the pathetic fallacy
do you?
think again
panpsychism is having its revival
as Whitehead said
all feeling is a lure for meaning
or did he say propositions are a lure for feeling?
whatever…

the ginkgo
is no slave to meaning
not condemned to meaning
takes no position on meaning
but assumes an absolute position
and does not give a shit
a human shit a dog shit
for what you say about meaning

but from our point of view
it is sad that the conversations
in bars have been shredded
ephemeral meanings decapitated

the street air is bare
around the ginkgo
we are driven indoors
and even outdoors hide our faces
our primate displays

thus abandoned by our talk
the ginkgo rare now in the wild
rescued by human cultivation
will outlast our dramas
outlast any given one of us
maybe all of us
oblivious to the nightly sirens
signifiers of the collective disaster
....

Tree chi
emergent from Chi'na
energetic / distilling rocks
human huts   pagodas
mountain snows
ancient towering groves

now here among the traffic lights
conducting the eye down the allée

see them turn in array
the gold framings*
punctuate their recession
green going to amber going to red
above the canopied frame
pale sky at dusk
below it the street
dark wet with rain
the ginkgos of Degraw
numinous   numerous
humanoid in their massed sociality
more European here
than Chinese
monumental in a uniform
march of bare trunks
dans un parc français
summative in their effect

indifferent to our comings and goings
from brunch
our philosophical bullshit
and requisite despair
(nu, is fascism on the way?
and what does the ginkgo have to say?)

Will the tree survive our madness?
all aesthetics
pushed out of form
gestalt become gevalt
tumult and destruct

ooh, ginkgo resist us
outpersist us will ya pleez?

it's spring / I have to sneeze

the ginkgos' cousins the sycamores
of elephant-limbed integument
are shedding their seeds
dust of zoo or savannah
clings to them too

A stroll with Linda
among these species
a comment here and there
on the strange speech of everything
and how we will fare
and what of the world for the offspring
we'll never know
about the grandkids
the sycamores or the rats in the park

the screen goes dark
universe congealed
vast opening in the existence-block
revealed

Vomit smell
of smashed fruit on the ground*
is alive
now from

the silver apricot gingko
female-seed manifests completely
sarcotesta and the soft
inside covered over
by a thin white
scleral layer

do not reject this odor
inhale it / accept it
Tientai teaching:
to fully manifest a thing
is to be liberated from it

No
to fully manifest
is to be liberated from liberation

Ah! the smell of vomit
like the piscine air
of female parts
smell of childbirth
between forms of excreta
all sweet all fully manifest
and the male seed hairy pollen
emitted by cones of the male tree
drifts on the breeze
enters the under-layer of the female
with motile sperm

and here we are
at the ecotone
of animal and vegetable
fallen off the ledge
of one-thing-is-just-itself
into the kingdom of context

it's life it's information
sent out across 290 million years
How long will it survive?
let's take bets
evidence: two venerable ginkgos
still alive a mile and a half from
ground zero Hiroshima
scarred and recovered
hah!
so what if seas rise
or fascist war turns a city
to rubble?

the ginkgo fully manifests
and when it's done it will have been
fully manifested
this will forever be the case
as is also with us

OK they last but
do they shit?
do they create waste
entropic energy transforms?

well yes yes the fanlike leaves
turn brown on the ground
and there is energy exchange
carbon in / oxygen out with some remainder
happening at an equal and opposite rate
to our own breathing, I think (must check this)
but otherwise their cycles of growth and decay
are much longer and their time sense
an attenuated Bergsonian durée

Consciousness drawn out / unmarked / unmeasured
beyond the moment beyond the day
a vague tailing off register
so let's hear it for the slow emergence
from the winking-in-and-out
of the quantum phenomenal level
existence is stretched in the mind of trees

and we are in the middle range
where again I must sneeze out
pollen that wants to mate with our kind
manifest it fully this wheeze
and merge with vomit smell* breeze

non-distinction
to fully
slow
down
and be the tree

which is to say
the gray air of today

dog shits
shouts
street fumes
looming societal collapse and threat

condensation on the brown
disconnected petals
unease
in the eye of the observer

Tolkien with his intuition
spoke the slow thoughts of Ents
to include and include and include

extremivore microbes
eating metal in the Gowanus incognito
and the ginkgo growing
on poisoned ground

look at Hiroshima
our human achievement
and the ginkgo likewise our creation
with something to teach
a magnificat of indifference

but AAAAH!
this riff is haunted

by the ghost of Joyce Kilmer
No No
keep god out of this
because we know
these
trees
fuck

yep
that's the way they roll
and they got soul
chi soul
but strangely I can't find
a single ginkgo image
in all my books of Chinese painting
pines yes plums yes
peach yes lotus yes
but ginkgo no
even though Chan and Taoist monks
cultivated and venerated them

in their nodular bones*
they do recall the ink-dot energies
of the High Tang and the Song
their bark clefts like splits
in the great gray cliffs

misty chi seams rising from the rock
masses of air implied
Cezanne-ian negativos

not used for furniture (much)
extract of ginkgo biloba
supposedly helps with insomnia
but not proven to work
and poisons if taken in excess

this is the useless tree
of Chan and Taoist lore
rarely cut down
a cultivar
in and for itself
inconsequential
non-utilitarian
but we value it
we love it

for its health
longevitay and
beautay

Notes

pg. 2 "The small ax" is after a tune by Bob Marley and the Wailers ("If you are a big tree, we are the small ax, sharpened to cut you down…").

pg. 3 "The chervil are dead…" is after a tune and skit by The Flight of the Conchords, "The Humans are Dead."

pg. 5 All references are to Alfred North Whitehead's *Process and Reality,* his major work of systematic metaphysics. Many years after the book was published, W. was asked by a student after one of his Harvard lectures what he meant by a certain passage in the book. W. paused to consider for a moment and then replied, "I have no idea."

pg. 20 Pyotr Kropotkin the late 19th/early 20th c. Russian left-anarchist/socialist whose treatise, *Mutual Aid,* made an argument for the primacy of intra-species cooperation over competition in the process of evolution. His was an argument against the social Darwinism of Spencer, et al. Darwin himself was more nuanced in his view of the relative importance of cooperation and competition, particularly focusing on inter-species accommodation and adaptation with his metaphor of the "tangled bank" of complementary flora (see reference on pg. 17). In this, he anticipated the concept of the ecosystem.

pg. 21 "The practico-inerte," a concept in the later Marxist thought of Jean-Paul Sartre that signifies the unintended, unforeseeable, and resistant consequences of social action.

pg. 22 Francis Ponge: 20th c. French prose poet whose books, such as *Taking the Side of Things (Le Parti Pris des Choses)*, are filled with close observations and thick descriptions of objects and processes natural and artifactual. His work is a particular favorite (an obsession, really) of mine.

pg. 23 "The True Man of No Rank" is a Chan Buddhist trope taken from Taoist sources and connotes the sage who neither seeks nor needs recognition.

pg. 24 "Old Roshi" Zen master Shunryu Suzuki: "we cut back the weeds and plant them…" (*Zen Mind, Beginner's Mind*).

QUILTED PILLOWS

pg. 25 "A series of dark, craggy pinnacles rises 80 metres above the grassy plains of Namibia. The peaks call to mind something ancient—the burial mounds of past civilizations or the tips of vast pyramids buried by the ages. The stone formations are indeed monuments of a faded empire, but not from anything hewn by human hands. They are pinnacle reefs, built by cyanobacteria on the shallow sea floor 543 million years ago, during a time known as the Ediacaran period. The ancient world occupied by these reefs was truly alien. The oceans held so little oxygen that modern fish would quickly founder and die there. A gooey mat of microbes covered the seafloor at the time, and on that blanket lived a variety of enigmatic animals whose bodies resembled thin, quilted pillows. Most were stationary, but a few meandered blindly over the slime, grazing on the microbes. Animal life at this point was simple, and there were no predators. But an evolutionary storm would soon upend this quiet world." Douglas Fox: "What Sparked the Cambrian Explosion?" *Nature* 2/10/2016.

pg.27 Deuterostomia are animals (sea horses, for example and many microorganisms) whose anuses form before their mouths in embryonic development.

pg. 28 Whitehead, with his concept of "objective immortality" (in my doubtless imperfect if not outright incorrect understanding), asserts that once an event happens, it will forever after be the case that it did so. Hence, the fact of its occurrence is immortal. Time and the forward development of the universe is, thus, built up on the pile of immortal corpses of fact.

pg. 29 Georg Trakl, the brilliant, mad early 20th c. Austrian poet who killed himself while serving in the Austrian army. His poems contain images of vegetal and mental/moral decay. *Verwirrt and wahnsinnig* are German words for confused and mad.

pg. 30 The bdelloid rotifer is a freshwater microorganism with a wheel-like array of cilia that sweep food into its rudimentary mouth. I get my information about this little critter from Richard Dawkins' wonderful book, *The Ancestor's Tale: A Pilgrimage to the Dawn of Time.*

pg. 32 Creode: a term of art coined by the English biologist C.H. Waddington, and signifying the developmental pathway of a cell as it grows to form part of a specialized organ. The import of this concept for me is that processes (Whitehead again, Tao and Zen) and not states of beings are fundamental.

pg. 35 Pythagoras: Greek pre-Socratic philosopher who believed that beans were sacred and to be avoided because they were empty and mirrored the form of the universe. Legend has it that he died at the battle of Marathon because he refused to run through a bean field to escape his attackers.

OPENINGS

pg. 39 The jeweled net of Indra in Vedic and Hua Yen Buddhist texts refers to the interconnection and interpenetration of everything. It bears a striking similarity to the 17th c. European philosopher Gottfried Wilhelm Leibnitz's concept of the monads, the infinite collection of entities that mirror each other and constitute the universe. (Link to the notion of quantum entanglement?)

CHINA

pg. 48 Burton Watson: preeminent translator and interpreter of classical Chinese and Japanese poetry, philosophy and Buddhist texts. I took his wonderful class on Chinese and Japanese poetry and translation many years ago at Barnard College (Columbia Univ.). Barbara Stoler Miller, a brilliant Sanskrit scholar, guest taught several class meetings and read from her translations of the erotic poetry of Jayadeva. Sadly, she died relatively young some years later.

pg. 51 *Wu shu*: martial art. *Wu wei*: a Taoist term translated variously as non-action; the action that is non-action; action without desire (Buddhist overtone there); empty action, etc.

SPRINGS

pg. 53 Monastir: a town in what is now North Macedonia whence my crazy Sephardic maternal forebears emigrated in 1915. They spoke an eastern Mediterranean mongrel dialect of Ladino, the 15th century Spanish of the Jews expelled from Spain in the Inquisition. Their speech was sprinkled with Greek, Turkish, Arabic, and Hebrew. Jizveh: a small brass coffee pot. Loukum: Turkish delight, a powdered candy. See *Return to Salonika* by Léon Sciaky, a fascinating and heartbreaking account of his revisit to

Salonika (where he had grown up), whose culturally rich Sephardic community was destroyed by the Nazis, and local Greek collaborationists in WWII.

"EVERYWHERE MEN SPEAK IN WHISPERS
I BROOD ON THE USELESSNESS OF LETTERS"

pg. 67 Han Shan : Cold Mountain poet and iconic Zen sage/fool/hermit of 8th (maybe 7th) c. China. Tu Fu: great poet of the High Tang, 8th c. China.

GINGKO AND FOOTNOTES

pg. 74 Wabi sabi: Japanese esthetic of age, transitoriness, and decay.

pg. 76 The pi-pa is an ancient Chinese lute. This move in Yang style Tai Chi is sometimes called Play Guitar. Left arm extends forward; right palm faces left elbow. Sounds harmless enough, but the martial art application is to apply opposing pressures to the opponent's arm and break it.

pg. 79 Panpsychism: everything is mind; everything is conscious.

pg. 83 Tien Tai: Chinese Buddhist doctrine and practice, precursor to Chan (Zen). *Being and Ambiguity* by Brook Ziporyn is an interesting contemporary application of Tien Tai principles to current Western philosophical problems

pg. 84 Ecotone: liminal zone where two or more ecosystems or forms of life meet and interpenetrate.

pg. 85 Henri Bergson: French philosopher of the late 19th and early 20th c. whose concepts of *elan vital* and duration, dismissed by many in the Anglo-American tradition of "scientific" philosophy, have had a lasting influence on Continental European thought. Basically (to vastly oversimplify) he is saying that experienced time cannot be reduced to quantifiable segments. Bergson and William James, the great American pragmatist, respected each other and carried on a correspondence.

NOTES

pg. 88 Poetry as the conduct of philosophy by other means, or the other way around.

Acknowledgements

A prior version of "The Coraçon Function" appeared in *Rat's Ass Review*.

Many thanks to my colleague, friend and co-conspirator, the poet Janet Kaplan, for her encouragement and expert reading and editing of this manuscript. These poems are vastly improved by her suggestions. Many thanks also to my longtime friend, the poet Bruce Kawin, for his encouragement and excellent suggestions.

Thanks also to Linda Schneider for her careful reading and editorial suggestions and to my psychotherapeutic colleague and friend Richard Bock for his encouragement of my work in poetry and in thinking and for our sharing of ideas.

About the Author

Peter Schneider is a poet and psychotherapist. Now retired from his therapy practice, he splits his time between Brooklyn, NY, and Rochester, VT. *In the Field of Unintended Consequences* is his second full-length collection. His debut collection, *The Map is Not the Territory*, was published in 2018 by Anaphora Literary Press.